A. 112

When I Kiss the Sky

WHEN I KISS THE SKY

ELIZABETH COOK

worple
press

First published in 2021 by
Worple Press
www.worplepress.co.uk

Printed by imprintdigital
Upton Pyne, Exeter
www.digital.imprint.co.uk

Typesetting and cover design by The Book Typesetters
us@thebooktypesetters.com
07422 598 168
www.thebooktypesetters.com

ISBN 978-1-905208-47-0

for David Cash

1942–2019

Acknowledgements

Elizabeth Cook's work includes fiction, poetry, and libretti. Her novel, *Lux* (Scribe), connects the Biblical story of David and Bathsheba with the 16th century poet, Thomas Wyatt. She is the author of the fiction, *Achilles* (Methuen and Picador USA), the poetry collection, *Bowl* (Worple), and a pamphlet, *The Sound of the Rain* (The Garlic Press). She has created the libretti for Francis Grier's oratorios, *The Passion of Jesus of Nazareth,* and *Before all Worlds*, the latter a Nativity setting. She has been a Hawthornden Fellow and was St Edmundsbury Cathedral's first Writer in Residence. She is currently a Fellow of the Royal Literary Fund. She grew up in Dorset and now lives in East London.

Thank you to the editors of the publications in which some of these poems were first published: *Conférence, Magma, MAP: Poems After William Smith's Geological Map of 1815, Moving Worlds, Poetry London, Scintilla, Stand, Tears in the Fence, The Backroad Journal, Theology, The Tree Line.* Many of the poems from The Garlic Press pamphlet have been included here. 'Edmund in Edmundsbury' was first published by St Edmundsbury Cathedral in a limited edition, hand-printed by the Jericho Press. 'The Saintes Maries de la Mer' has been set to music by Judith Bingham; 'The Elephant Tree' and the two bandstand poems were written as part of a song cycle, *In the Park*, with music composed by Francis Grier. 'Memory House' won First Prize in the 2020 Crabbe Poetry Competition; 'Calf' won Third Prize in the 2020 Troubadour International Competition.

Particular thanks to those friends who have read and commented on my poetry – David Black, Robert Chandler, Diana Hendry, Martha Kapos, Paul Mills, and Hamish Whyte – and to fellow members of the East Suffolk Poetry Workshop. I have been fortunate in my editors, Michael Laskey (who edited the earlier pamphlet) and Peter Carpenter being among the very best.

Heartfelt thanks to Sienna Anderson for her breathtaking photograph of the egret.

Contents

Exemplum

(for Samuel SSF)

She might have flown in a different way
if she had not been hungry.
What we marked
during the fifteen or so minutes while she crossed
and recrossed the air that lay above us
was her diligence, never altering
the tempo of her flight.
Thorough as a woman
going over a length of fabric
searching for slubs and weaknessses;
unhurried as the tractor that crawls up
and down its field of heavy clay,
then from side to side, turning it over
clod by buttery clod,
till the whole field is refashioned and gleams,
rearticulated. New-known.

So the red kite persisted.
Her urgent hunger
and the hunger of her young
never for a moment provoking her to rush
or carelessness. What Eckhart calls the *evenness* of God
made plain in the raptor's patient, consistent attention
to every inch of this rough, knotted ground.

Lupa

The first litter had been unerring.
No sooner had she licked them clean,
eaten the slippery membrane, than they found their way
to a teat, sucked themselves strong;
at times gnawed at her
till she was raw.

These big bald ones really hadn't a clue.
They made a noise that her milk could stop
but they did not know how to find the milk.
She developed a way of arranging her limbs,
keeping her claws sheathed, to support and cradle
the babies, who also wrapped arms
round each other.

Yet because they pulled down her milk
they were hers. She would keep them.
When the first man came she went for his throat,
snarled to protect her incompetent young.
They clung together, preferred the safety of her shelter
to that of the tall noisy creature
who claimed them.

Then four men came. They carried the carcass
of a sheep which they flung down some distance away,
meaning to distract her.
She looked over there,
raised her muzzle and scented the air.
Her ears showed that she almost heard
the meat call. But she stayed.

So the men took her out with an arrow,
then speared her. The last the boys knew
of their foster mother was the noise of her howling,
as she scrabbled with her paws to defend them,
to save herself, and the savage
hills that were home.

Thinking of Thomas Hardy

i. The Fieldfare

The fieldfare was all skin and bone:
He held the dead bird in his hand.
His father killed it with a stone.
The fieldfare was all skin and bone –
a creature in whom life had shone
though chilled and starved. So bare the land,
the fieldfare was all skin and bone.
He held the dead bird in his hand.

★

He never could forget how light the dead bird was,
        nor, knowing of it now, can I.
It rested on his palm like a ball of fine-blown glass
        that a breath could lift away.

ii. The Biscuit Tin

He wished to be buried in Stinsford churchyard
Next to his Emma, the wife re-beloved,
But his body was taken in pomp to Westminster
And only his heart was interred next to her.

And what contriving it took to get even that there:
A surgeon fetched in to cut the thing out.
It was wrapped in a towel like pie for a neighbour
Then sealed in a tin to be safe from the cat.

How very odd! How macabre! To think of your heart
Where the biscuits had been – 'crumb-outcaster' with crumbs!

Both grotesque and sad – as the stories you wrote
Where recalcitrant stuff often baffles intention
(Tess's letter to Angel lost under the mat) –
That most unsettled heart laid to rest in a tin.

Note on The Biscuit Tin

What if the cat did make away with the heart
(as the word went in the Dorchester pubs)?
Would he have cared? He might have enjoyed
the idea of his flesh being food for his friend?
Metempsychosis – the poems are full of it –
men and women into plants and trees. Why not a cat?
He'd tried a beard and moustaches before
but never a tail and complete coat of fur.

Orrery

i.m. Aletta Seymour 1970–2008

that day we made the orrery
you asked to be the moon
but the moon was already spoken for
so instead you settled on Neptune

and went to the edge of the garden
and climbed the flint wall to the lane
till we no longer saw you do planetary motion
as we turned
  turned in the rain

The Elephant Tree

(for Elle B)

When we go to the park we run
to our elephant tree.
There's a whorl in the wood
like an elephant eye; the bark is rough
like an elephant's skin, and the trunk
of the tree dips low,
almost touching the ground.

We sit on it and swing our legs and stroke
our elephant's trunk. We do not run unless we think
we hear him bellow.

The Young Palaeontologist: Lyme Regis 1808

She looks down at her feet in the slippy clay
as the sea puddles round them. When she steps away
these soft-edged pools become shallow
and fade.

She bends over, becomes quadruped,
palms set in the wet greensand.
Were she to linger, would the impression
endure; mould her in stone? She has seen
how a creature can be changed in its nature:
sucked dry, packed down to mineral.

She has watched her father strip mussels from a post
as if they were brussel sprouts; she has watched
those mussels as the sea slooshes over them – how they gape,
showing their buds of meat like tongues.
She has also seen them pursed up and dry – no longer animal
– with something like mortar
squeezed from their closure.

Too young to be entrusted with a knife,
she employs the fine, calcified edge
of an oyster shell, makes it a blade
to prise away limpets, winkles, whelks.
They clatter like clinker in her bucket.

She scours rock pools for the lives they harbour:
sea vegetable fronds, crabs and the tender
blobs of jelly that might sting her if she prods them.
She finds ridged snails turned into stone,
so cleanly cased in their lias bed, they're like kidneys
fresh from the butcher, glistening intact

in the cold surrounding fat her mother pulls away
to render down to oil.

She lifts a large rounded stone – pale grey,
she knows its kind – and cradles it
as she would a cat, before letting it fall and split.
Displayed at its heart, neat as the print
of bird feet or script,
a thing that is vertebrate.

Up

Now I see you. Now
I don't, as you dip
in and out of the field
of my vision, a child
swinging between columns,
into the folds of the shadows
of a long, cool arcade.
For a moment you're a waterbird
that dives clean
under the waves;
then, as a porpoise,
you thread those waves
(and the waves are thick, and the waters
they crown are deep);
and next you're a girl again,
yellow hair loosened,
running through a field of stooked corn,
running down the narrow parting
between rows (though it's rough
and scratchy with weeds and stumps
and scattered grain); you run
till the high stooks swallow you
leaving me standing
on high, open ground.

The grass is silent.
The wide moor with its patchwork of bracken and heather is silent.
Only near the yellow gorse
are bees, steady at their divination. Their hum
more vibration than sound.

Then indisputable song,
from the tiny dot of a lark that is rising, music
squirling from the roped
waters of her throat as she moves,
with unerring direction up
into a fathomless sky.

Pesci diversi

What luxury to visit fish in Florence!
The aquarium so much less crowded than the Pitti
or the Uffizi – fewer exhibits; far fewer visitors.
I almost swim between the tanks myself.
My eyes, refreshed and educated
by Giotto, Angelico, and Lippi,
delight in this liquidity and glow,
the luminous colours,
the fishes' flowing tails; their silent whiskings
and turnings. After so many chapels –
Brancacci, Pazzi, Medici –
this pulsing, glugging penumbra
invites reverence.

From tank to tank I make a quiet progress
and rest at each in contemplation,
as at a Station of the Cross.
Obediently I scan each group description
identifying every living item
in terms of genus, species, habitat:
Apolemichthys xanthopunctatus, the Gold-spangled
Angel fish; *Gobiodon histrio*;
Siganus unimaculatus:
the Clown Goby,
the One-spot Fox-face.

– a kind of litany, although the Latin
cannot begin to contain
these subtle, translucent beauties
that drift and slip, dart and ride in reveries
no label can illuminate or mind guess.
The octopus skulks unmoved by its nomenclature.
The flat fish lie like flayed pelts on the floor,

then lift and stir into swift shivers
as if a draught from elsewhere had passed through.

At the final station a handwritten card
reads only 'Pesci Diversi': and here
an undetermined quantity of fish
untroubled by their namelessness
continue to explore their liquid space
or press – in what might be reciprocal interest –
their mouths against the glass.

Was this apology for a label
the product of ignorance or exhaustion?
I hope it was rebellion:
the taxonomist, confounded
by such beautiful diversity.
Let them swim
– thought she or he –
in their unnamed particularity
beyond the narrow corridors of species
into an infinite heaven of resemblances
with clowns and angels, foxes
and many-sequinned dancers;
with all that moves,
with all that has colour and mood

The Bandstand by Day

Seen from afar
it's an empty birdcage
– doors flung open,
prisoners free.

Yet birds do perch
on its apex finial,
a fat seagull
like a weather vane,

or the lake's heron
will stand quite still,
his long bill
casting a gnomon shade.

The Bandstand by Night

Each night, when the park is locked, men
and women squeeze through gaps
in the railings, or clamber across them,
thinking themselves unseen.

Some seek out thickets of trees;
others climb the hill to the bandstand
and make love beneath its cupola
as if on an altar.

Their cries and their murmurs
are a music far
from that of the spreading fanfare
of brass that once rang here:

the trombones, the horns and the cymbals;
the euphonium and sweet cornets –
how they brightened the air with their lustre!
How they lift and order the listeners' hearts !

Dürer, 1514: Two Studies

i Melencolia 1

The starved hound shivers in his sleep
while in his dream he bounds like the hare
he's been chasing through hedge-gaps,
across rimed ridges, bright in the moon. While she,
gravid with thought, dreams of when stone
was a flatness on the palm that could skim
the unwrinkled level of a lake or a still sea,

not this polyhedron, unrollable:
kerlunk kerlunk, facet after facet.
Her garment is thick bombazine,
freighted with loops and fastenings
for keys and sundries. The sand
in the upper chamber of the hourglass drills,
mining the mound it builds.

ii St. Jerome

The lion and the dog are snoozing together
as the prophet almost foretold. Sunlight, filtered
through chequer-board
of thick-lensed panes,
caresses a skull that's as companionable
and casual as a doffed hat on a shelf.

Scratch scratch. Scratch scratch.
Dip and flick of nib in ink pot. The saint hears only
the words in his mind. Pursues
only the Word.
In the hour-glass the soft sand falls,
lands on its cushion of sand.

Gust

When she considers how long it has been
since another person's large, tobacco-soaked
tongue has occupied her mouth she remembers
the time when their dog picked up the ball
of a curled-up hedgehog and could not get it out
of her soft mouth so they had to prise it
free – all those spines – till both creatures
were separate again and the hedgehog
made off with surprising speed while the dog panted,
slack-jawed and salivating, her whole nature burning
from the recent, astonishing conjunction.

Les Saintes Maries de la Mer

(or how the Gospel was brought to the Camargue)

Mary Jacobus and Mary Salome
were thrust in a boat with no oar and no sail
and pushed out to sea
along with Sarah
their servant from Africa.
How did they dare?

What did they carry
in that small boat's hold
for their uncertain journey?
I hope they took figs
to sustain them, and honey, plus skins
and skins full of water.

For how many days
did that small world drift
on a full-bellied tide (pulled by currents
through storms)? They had surely lost track
when their boat ran aground in a land of low winds
and endless salt marsh.

But not missing a beat
they climbed from the boat
and dragged it ashore
where they rolled up their sleeves:
there was work to begin,
a story to tell.

Rain

'this loose girdle of soft rain' – Hart Crane

I can imagine, one day, out of this world,
missing the sound of the rain,
the thick wet bees of it, rushing arpeggios;
cadences
of fingerfall.

It was good in the hut
where the corrugated iron
of the roof made a drum.
Lovely too are rain–
blown craters in sand,

like those on the face
of another planet,
seen from afar.

Listen! the rain enfolding us here.

Edmund in Edmundsbury

I

It was not yet dawn when the boy
and the bishop climbed the mild hill
beyond Bures. A moon – near to full –
cast long shadows across grass
and ploughed furrows. They saw hares
bounding for cover, were accompanied
by the soft shudderings of owls, first
fidgetings in the hedges.
They watched sky pale and sun rise
on Christmas morning. The year eight hundred
and fifty six.

The boy knelt. The bishop poured holy oil
on his brow and a new king stood.
Edmund, a man now, saw his kingdom spread out
like an ample robe at his feet, lit by God's sun.
He put the robe on.

And wore it. Never forgetting the light
of the Son in whose light he lived and for whom
he lived. Dearer than life
was that light, his own life a mirror
reflecting that light through his realm of East Anglia –
clearer by far than the light of the flames
of the Danes who scorched it, injured
that kingdom with trespass and taking.

The year now eight seventy.
Bound to an oak tree, bristling with arrows
each puncture a mouth from which not only blood flows
but gift to his people, witness of faith.

It flows out through the rivers, the Dove and the Nene
the Stour and the Waveney, Linnet and Lark
the Yare and the Wensum,
the Gipping, the Wissey,
Ouse Great and Little; the Colne
– all the conflowing waters
of holy East Anglia – they bear trace of his bleeding,
their silt fed by his dying, as he called to his Lord.
Lord Jesus, to you Lord, to you Lord alone
I surrender my life. Lord keep my folk faithful
Better my death than a land turned to Odin.

His mouth went on calling, his wounds went on bleeding.
Nothing stopped either, the Danes could not bear it.
They swept off his head, but still it kept crying,
ceaselessly called to its One Lord and Saviour.
Those cries sounded taunts to the Danish destroyers
– having sliced off the head, they kicked it away
far out of earshot for the saint's prayers offended,
lessened their triumph in slaying this king.

II

Where is he now? Toulouse's St Sernin?
Here under the tennis courts – or next door
at St Mary's? A chapel at Arundel?
Let's ask the head that the wolf
safely-guarded, protected from harm
with claw-sheathed paws
while good men toiled through brambles
(clothes stained with blackberries)
cupping their ears, straining to hear
that holy head as it cried (never stopping)
Here and *Here* and *Here*…

Hic et ubique?..
Here and everywhere.

Guard it, wolf. Guard it safely
this head of a king, a crowned king,
as the jewel of your soul.
You scatter the demons, you keep it in safety.
Virtue's friend.

III

Heaped at the lane-side like heads lopped in warfare
the sweet sugar-beet on its way to the factory.
From strength issued sweetness, honey in bones,
a riddle for Samson.

From the factory chimney the sweet smoke puffs,
rides the sky like the cartoon smoke
of a chuffa train in a picture book. Or else,
like a pennant – horizontal
merrily waving to announce the lists.
Beodricesworth.
Edmundsbury: home to the Greene King,
burial ground of the martyr king –
his body stowed: better than any gold hoard.

This flat land is shaped
by towers: to hold men in
and keep men out.
To climb towards God
or make a show of trying.

This new tower welcomes: its four corners from a distance
like newell posts, or thumb and forefinger
from each hand held

23

for the windings of celestial thread, angelic
cat's cradle; made of the stone
of East England: Lincolnshire Barnack,
Peterborough gypsum.

In our intercessions tonight we pray most especially
for the flower arrangers
and the coffee makers
and all the churches throughout the world dedicated
to our patron, Edmund.

IV

Come first to the garden
where everything happened
– Creation, separation,
agony, prayer. Burial
and resurrection.
And where everything continues to happen – Alan
head of Groundforce, understands this.
Twice as many pass through these grounds
as venture beneath the roofed spaces
of the Cathedral.
The soil has a record of human passing – fragments
of Roman tiles, a rare coin
from 1600, clay pipes, bullet cases
made of brass, remnants
of recent war. Might it also
contain trace – a chip of bone,
a ribbon of DNA –
of that revered body
buried nearby, so lovingly tended
(nails and beard trimmed,
the clippings retained

for miraculous action)? The soil
stays rich. Keeps mum.

The Bury Herball lives
in rosemary, rue, and thyme,
the various and variegated sages
that grow here. Visitors
who move through the herb garden finger
the leaves, and leave
with a scent unchanged
since the monks of the Abbey grew
their medicinal simples.
                              The gardeners
have their ministry of welcome.
Ada! There's a man on his knees here!
When was the last time you saw
a man on his knees?
                      Just look
inside the Cathedral, Ada.
There are more men
on their knees in there.
Come inside.

V

So much for Martha and her people to do.
Let us pray for her
as she polishes the wood, the brass, the silver.
Washes and irons the altar linen,
checks the inverted candelabras
of Stephen Dykes Bower,
replaces spent bulbs.
The light requires a great deal
of human help to shine.

And as we pray
spare a thought – a prayer – for those
who stitched the kneelers
we kneel on. One or two
for almost every parish
in Suffolk – Shelley the latest.
(At a new canon's installation
a kneeler from home
will attend that canon's knees
– a small, seldom noticed, miracle
contrived by a careful verger.)

This building is fabric – as Lenny
the one and only maintenance man
knows only too well,
as do Stephen and Keith
(tuner and tuner's
assistant at Harrison
and Harrison, organ makers
and organ maintainers of distinction).
Each month they climb the steep,
narrow stairs to the loft.
For hours they tap and listen. Careful
as dental hygienists, or surgeons,
their work minute, precise,
a listening to the air
stop after stop – *Bourdon,*
Lieblich, Quintana,
Vox Humana –
while it clarifies,
clears to a note that's true.

High in the loft the organist – a rodeo
rider of distinction – straddles the great breath-
filled creature, reaches the wide-
spaced stops, plies pedals till sound

floats out and swells
to fill sanctuary, chancel, aisles:
the whole nave washed
by a mighty sea.

The nave is a ship
and the ship's on the sea
and the whole sea
is in the ship,
at its helm
the governor (*gubernator:*
pilot or steersman, or in this case,
steerswoman).

We pray also for our choristers
and give thanks to God
for the gift of music...

In the Song School
beneath a coffered ceiling
choristers listen to the silence

between

two

words.

What is the difference –
they are asked to consider –
between *forever* and *for*
ever?

No silence on Tuesday evenings
when the bellringers practise
(*We thank you, Lord, for their office*)

but at 12.30 every Thursday
in the Lady Chapel
there is a silence to sit in
while eyes rest on Goff's carving
of Mother and Child,
she calmly restraining
– or is she simply blessing? –
her endlessly
surprising boy.

And as if continuing the story
on the other side of the sanctuary,
in the same pale wood, by the same sculptor, Edmund,
king and martyr, his life and death witness
to the life of that mother's child.

Is he here? Here in this wood? What part of him
shines from the face of that serious boy king?
Does he dwell also in the cast metal
of Frink's warrior – his noble aspect turned away
as if in disdain of the self-saving bargain
proposed by the Danes?

VI

Let us pray also for the concert stewards, the volunteers
who staff the shop and the library.
We pray for the welcomers
and for our learned guides…

Two women – a mother and daughter –
after a day well spent at the Arc,
drop in for some culture.
They're taken on a thorough tour
and see details they would never have noticed unaided –

more than they'd bargained for.
As they move into the cloister, the weary mother
turns to her daughter. *What a lot to take in!*
I did like the mouse by the pulpit.
Who would have thought it! But let's get some tea.
I could murder a Danish.

Let them go on to the Refectory
to Cabinet Cake and tea, while we remember
the real and mutual slaughter
of Danes and East Anglians in nearby Thetford
(the Danes' base that long-ago winter)
and captured Edmund's valour.
What was it all for?

It's clear that the story is not yet over,
may never be.
The answer to *Where is he?* may simply be
that the question dissolves.
When a loved friend dies
those qualities you once admired in that person
need new homes. We living ones must take them on.
So Edmund's virtues: steadfastness,
courage, a looking to Christ,
self-sacrifice, valour – flew out with his life
to seek new men and women to uphold and act them.

When our prayers concern Edmund are they *for* him,
or through him? I think we pray *with* him;
and as we do, throughout his kingdom –
the realm of East Anglia –
that crowned head of Edmund
(*weorþfull cyning*, holy saint)
in its many locations –
on carved ends of benches,
roof bosses and statues,

stitched in wool,
and painted on canvas,
in jewel-coloured glass of sun-pierced
windows, at the foot of the Bishop's cathedra in Bury
 – so variously imaged it cries out
as one: *Here I am*
I am here.

Fox, you've changed

You who to me were splendid
– a Hilliard boy
upon a ground of flame,
the glorious eidolon
fox, glimpsed
at street corners
in the privacy of night
to whose folds you returned;
always a gift,
a revelation –
have become
a brazen lout,
tipping up
with your friends, your litter
of cartons, smeary with sauces,
in the garden, in daylight.
Rowdy picknickers,
loose limbed, shameless,
you have dug up my darling,
eaten his flesh, played spillikins
with his cleaned bones,
and still you dare
return my gaze.

The Assignment

'Deep assignments run through all our lives' – J. G. Ballard

It was Lurgan Sahib, the Healer of Sick Pearls,
who set fifteen or so crystals on a tray, let Kim
and the Hindu boy examine them awhile,
handle them if they would, before he covered
the stones with a paper and asked, first Kim
and then the other, to describe them
in as much detail as they could recall.

Kim was able to cite their number
and generic colour. The other boy,
Kim's rival, recalled every aspect, every differentiating
feature. The weight, colour and provenance
of each stone. There is *a four ruttee sapphire*
chipped at the edges,
one Turkistan turquoise, plain
with black veins, and there are two inscribed –
one with the name of God in gold,
and the other being cracked,
for it came out of an old ring
I cannot read.

As children we played a simple version:
a tray laid with a miscellany of objects:
thimble, matchbox, a propelling pencil, a key
and usually a cotton reel.
About twenty in all
and five minutes to remember them.

The present assignment is harder:
to unpack myself and spread out before me
things that have no names: ill-formed,
clumped together like metal
fused into odd conjunctions by the great heat

when the bomb fell,
or like pieces of coal where maybe a beautiful fossil
pokes through a sheer facet.

The task is to look at these ungainly things
for as long as it takes, until they're familiar,
consider them with a wide, kindly attention
that allows their internal structure to loosen
and spread, perhaps flower like the petals
of tight, apparently petrified, buds.
Poor pieces that would otherwise clatter into the kidney dish
like shrapnel at an autopsy.

The Leopard Leapt

Though the man had kept his wits about him
and always carried a gun,
the leopard leapt and fell on him
while he walked through the narrow pass.

The leopard leapt and fell on him,
clung fast to the man's back;
sunk its teeth in at the hairline,
and draped itself like a cloak.

The leopard leapt and hung on
till its head had become the man's crown
and the enormous paws draped over the shoulders
were fancy epaulettes.

The man with paws for epaulettes
carried the beast like a pelt.
When the leopard died the pelt grew thin
and lay like a map on the man's skin:

those few who saw him naked said
the birth-mark was strange and extensive.
But there was one whose touch he craved;
she found the birth-mark compelling.

At intimate moments she'd kiss it
and lap it with her tongue,
devote herself to a ridge with an edge
and worry at it to make it lift.

Perplexed by such searching arousal
he fingers the flap of skin;
and with exquisite pain he peels it free.
See the pelt of the raw man!

Stripped of his skin the man dies
but the woman bears him a son.
When the son becomes man her advice is
that he always carry a gun.

The Boy who Hurts Trees

There's a tree with arms
uplifted, in supplication
or praise or, as a toddler
who lifts up his arms, obedient
to the mother who will come
to shimmy off his vest
or pyjamas; haul him
out of the cooled bath.

Tall and pale as a peeled tree himself,
he comes in the blank hours
of afternoons, before schools
have emptied, when only a woman
and her dog might cross
his path, eyes low,
scouring the ground.

Often he is weaponless,
using the might
of a steel-capped boot
to kick the tree, repeatedly,
till the bark ruptures.
Then he'll swing on a bough and make it sag,
twist and wrestle it to the ground
to leave a jagged stump.

But sometimes he'll take out a knife
and stab his tree, wounding the bark
till he's able to claw some off with his fingers.
Then, again with the knife, he'll hack
at the pulp, *Bad tree. That'll teach you.*

Boy, under what bed
do you lay your fine boots? In what drawer
do you close up your knives?
Between what sheets – if any – do you sheathe
that bare body of yours?

Approximate

Distal, proximal, anterior, sagittal —
these cool words — how they anneal
the hot metal of the suffering
that we plunge into them,
causing a brief sizzle.

So Marie Curie described the burns
that seemed to come from the inside — *medial*
to the epidermis — so strangely
flushed with them.

When all is said,
approximation
is closest. Staying near. Leaning:
a small elephant into the side
of his mother; a swan
patrolling the place where a stone struck her mate;
and now, at your bedside, obedient
to what ineluctably draws nearer,
next to you. As near as can be.

arrest

It's a minefield out there. Here.
The manifold occasions to stop. This dead tree
for instance – blanched, upended,
all roots exposed and sand-scrubbed. In their intricate
arrangement and appearance they're like bones – they frame space
for vessels to pass through, as bone might
the arteries and nerves of the pelvis or in this case, air
that streams through the tree's fine foramina.

In this one piece of flotsam, there is enough
for a lifetime of expertise and absorption.

The wind lifts the surface of the sand
and chases it, skittering forward,
a restless, shifting commentary
to the grave bass of the land.

Memory House

When nouns – proper and common –
began to go, she remembered
Giordano Bruno,
his memory theatres
by means of which an orator
might recall the propositions
of a speech, and place sentences
in key positions such as a pediment,
architrave, or column, within
an imagined theatre.
                       She would use
her childhood home
which she could not shake off
and adorn it with entities
and situations
of greater fragility –

fireplace, kitchen sink, flagstones
in the larder; coal cellar,
woodshed, the kitchen
window where the cat
came in. The bookcase
on the upstairs landing –

she would tie what she wanted
to remember to these solid
locations as some tie prayers
and wishes to a tree, making the
fastening firm with a double bow.
There. The name of a long ago lover
tied to the mantelpiece, and there
the town in Sardinia where someone
– was it she? – fell over and grazed

40

her knee as a child might do
and the woman from the cake shop
ran out with a chair and a slice
of a tart made with apricots
ranged beautifully
like roof tiles.

Talking with Eric

The glass in the arcade slot machine
held rings, china toys, diamante bracelets,
and always a tiara;
a small chest marked
with skull and crossbones.
When we fed in a coin a mechanical arm
moved to select and deliver a gift,
unless the grabber failed.

I watch as your mind hovers,
like the little crane in the cabinet,
over one item of treasure
and then another, to select
and close upon what must appear
a manageable gift. I watch as you haul that gift
over to the chute at the front of the apparatus
– the place where the glass wall separates us –

but the chosen thing is so heavy and the teeth
of the contraption so flimsy
I fear that the hold cannot hold.
I will it to land perfectly
and see that you also are willing it
to arrive where you aim it; for it to be exactly,
to be the very thing
that this moment between us requires.

As Told by Ramakrishna

A man – or a woman, let us call her Hazel –
consulted a sage to ask, 'How long,
how many years, till I am wise
and become one with the All?'

'As many years,' the sage replied,
'as there are leaves on this great oak
we stand below.' 'So many!' gasped Hazel,
and away she went, sorrowful.

Another – Faizel perhaps – consulted the sage.
'How many years, O wise one, till I achieve
that annihilation of self in the greater radiance
of truth, that is the destiny of all?'

'As many years,' came the answer,
'as there are grains of sand within this desert
where we dwell.' A sense of rapture flooded Faizel.
He was heard to breathe 'So few!'

and directly, in that moment, was enlightened.

pulse

flawless sky
withdraws
by small sips
invaginates
to make a path
Is that where you go?

blackbird
spills out
beak so yellow
so entirely
midline against black
All here

A Whole Glade

She dreamt that his chest, his warm chest
pressed close to her back while they slept
was a whole glade, springy and thick
with bluebells.
               Any ill
she had recently entertained
in her thoughts about him was dispelled
for a while, subdued
by that dream with its after-scent
and the sight of the dent
like a form in grass
that their one shape made.

Token

(Antipaxos, 1986)

Because the island has no natural harbour
   And no one had made one,
I swam across to the beach
   When the boat dropped anchor.

Smooth and chalky – eggs from a giant hen –
   Stone upon stone, a stack of them,
Hot to my feet just cooled by the water,
   Bright in the sunshine.

At the edge, swagged honeysuckle, sweet-scented and thick.
   I broke off a sprig and furled my lips
To cover my teeth while I clamped on it, waded out
   To swim and climb back to you, watching from the deck.

I hope to arrive with another such token –
Pungent sample from here – should I make it to heaven.

Lift

When she was five
she made a tissue paper butterfly
and placed it on a fuschia bush whose flowers
were dancing ladies in pink skirts and men
in brilliant tails.
On the tissue she inscribed
a tiny letter to her grandmother
recently and incomprehensibly
deceased. The paper was so thin
and the shape of it so winged that the air
would surely lift it, carry it aloft,
up into the heaven she believed
was even finer.

The Night Bus

When we walk
you're on my right
as when we sit
and watch the telly
your left hand wedged
between my thighs
to keep it warm
and keep it safe
         Lately
with your knee so bad
I'd stand
to the left of you
braced
to take the weight off you
as you gripped
my right hand
for each turfy step down
from that high tor
near to Old Town
and to keep you
from slipping
on the scrambled
descent
to where the waterfall
pools
at Inversnaid
         And in bed
you're on my left
as a chair
on which I perch
until I turn
and carry you
'All aboard'

Ting Ting
Sit tight

Thus we ride
into the night

At Dark-Break

The brown stood out against the cypress' green:
a dry dead leaf, caught in the mesh of a tree.
Then a breeze tipped it, showed the stippled bloom
of a moth's pale pelt, two wings stroked so close
they made a single sail.

I sat with it an hour, wondering if it lived;
it hung so perfectly still, like its own hat
hung on a peg in a quiet corner
of an active house.
                    When I came back
an hour on it was as still, wings now

a little parted – as if an oyster knife
had slid between, or someone had breathed
apart two leaves of smoothed-together tissue.

Throughout the afternoon, whenever I returned
I found the angle wider, till it showed
the soft, private fur
of the hinge that formed the body,
and the great, unseeing eyes
like rust-rimmed targets on each wing.

Through day to dusk an opening:
each wing a sensor for the freight
of dark the day held pursed
like molecules of moisture.
                    When I went out
that night the moth had flown, for dark had filled
and spread those eyed and ragged wings
till they were wide and strong to meet it,
lift and beat the warm night air.

'I am usually vigilant'

I am usually vigilant
but when, last night,
you'd slid
from the bed,
I woke embracing
a bunched
-up heap
of linen.

It was after
the dream
in which
however hard
I clung
to the satisfactory
barrel of your body
it shrunk

away, slim
as a snake,
then a thread,
until from a slender
seedling's filament
it thinned
and could no more
be found.

Stealth

a hand
gloved in black leather
snips
through
each supply cable in turn
with a neat nip
of the pliers

This was the devil
cruel and deft
leaving her
apparently as before
but in fact cut off
and though motionless
utterly utterly adrift

The Candles

'The longer she stands, the shorter she grows', Nursery Rhyme

Through all of the dark day they burnt together –
the two thick squat ones, the tall pale taper.
But when night fell I found
that the taper was gone:
not a snout of wick
not a drop of wax left,
just the empty pewter holder where Miss Netticoat stood
tall and lovely in her white petticoat.

Peacock Season

Throughout these wide March days
the boards and narrow sills
of this old house are stationed by the sails
of peacock butterflies.

A slow whisk whisk. Lazy,
infrequent. Audible only
at the margins of hearing. They're
waking from their winter sleep.

Thus they sleep: upright, wings
sealed, the bright targets
of the eyes enclosed to show
the modest, sooty undersides.

Open   Shut   Open   Shut: the leaflets
of their wings breathe peacefully.
But it's too cold for them to live outside
and if they take off here they'll fly indoors

and stun themselves to death against the panes.
I learn to lift them onto my thumb's edge
– with what docility they climb and cling
while I transport them to an open shed.

Alas that single wings
lie scattered on the floor.
Torn petals, velvet shreds
of pansies. Dark confetti.

Duck, just inches from the back door

but well concealed.
Rarely does she leave
her nest and so uncover
the ten white eggs
she's laid there.

Her plumage
of several browns
continues and resembles
the differing tones
of the dry flaking stem
of lavender
she's nested under.

I make her into an emblem
of fortitude
and patience,
and while she guards
and warms her eggs believe
that I guard her – my breath and feet
quiet when I'm near.

A dark intelligent eye
locks onto my gaze.
I can't tell if she fears or trusts
the creature that it sees,
or what it takes for her to stay.

The Ascent of Gulliver

When they pinned you down, my Gulliver,
secured you with ropes, thick ones, tied to rocks
so you could not rise up, I made myself
Lilliputian and climbed

all over you, inspected each inch
of your warm, springy flesh. I turned ant
and scampered across your surfaces,
then as bee thrust myself down

into the calyces of your ears,
to taste the bitter gold
of the wax; as dung beetle
rolled into boulders the flecks of shit

that lay neglected in the crack
of your bum. I wanted to know
every inch of the terrain: the salt
in your lachrymal ducts, the comforting

scent of your balls, like whey;
the soft skin under them. I loved it
that you stayed – patient, obedient –
loved the fact you were not in any

position to leave. But you left.
In a moment of my inattention, your life
lifted, as a flock of birds
who all day long have been feeding

on the revealed goods
of a ploughed field,
will suddenly
rise up as one and fly off

and all you can hear
is the whirr of their wings,
a skirmish of air,
and they're gone

Folds

Do you remember those clacker-boards
like table-tennis bats with a weight swinging
from a string below;
and a little family of hens peck pecking –
heads that bobbed in unison
as they set to their feast
of invisible corn?

They were like that, this family
in their square bed, each of the four edges occupied
by a row of heads on pillows,
– the narrow, hairless chests of the men
(all so pale I could not tell which
of their number it was that was dying) –
when the orderlies pulled them all out here
to be together on the infirmary flagstones.

                              'This,' I thought,
as I lay in my own small bed at the edge
of the pavement, wanting to stay snug,
wanting not to intrude or to leave,
'This is the way. To die with the whole family
in bed beside you, their warm toes
touching your cold ones.' And then when all's done
the bed plucked up
like a chequered picnic cloth; or folded,
corners to middle into origami squares,
turned over and folded again, corners
to middle, to make a lotus flower, or a contraption
worked with your fingers to tell fortunes on.

in Rembrandt's studio

a candle and an angel
an open window
                    a lit
fire
            the one currency
is light

Draw only what you see

undress

As she goes
down the corridor
of arched hawthorn
and field
maple one
by one
she disposes
of hat
scarf
and gloves

Next her coat
and the dress
the slip
and the small
lacy pieces
she steps from
and drapes
each item
across
a branch
or a twig
as if passing
them into
the hands
of a servant
to fold
or to store

We were familiar
with the place
as the haunt
of nightingales

in summer
and go often
ourselves
on warm
evenings
to listen

When we reached
there it looked
as if romany
washing
had been hung
on the hedgerows
to dry
or get sweet
from contiguous
blossom

The shed clothes
were without
any air
of violation
though we thought
it probable
a girl
had gone in
to the dark
as she might
from an empty beach
enter
the night
sea and swim
out with no light
but spangles
of phosphorous

If Jesus Came to My House
(for J N)

The book's long gone but the title
was enough. Now I would settle
for Mum or Dad back here for the afternoon.
Something as usual as tea together
would be so wide with marvels I think
I might die of the gladness.

But I'd need to take care not to drown
in that gladness, contain it in small,
modest enquiries, *Are you warm enough?*
Another cup?
And all the time my heart careening,
crazy, yelping with love.

With you it's different since you're here,
if only (you've been led to believe)
for a short while longer. When we meet
we grip hands across the table and pretend
not to notice we're trying to make the impress
of a body's weight permanent

as we talk, in the way we have talked for more
than forty years, of books, birds, and music, poems and paintings,
of the sweet light in Watteau's *les plaisirs du bal*
which to Constable seemed to have been painted
by a brush dipped in thin honey
and almost a miracle.

Quilt

He had expected,
when death came near,
to be too full of terror
for the process to go well.
He pictured himself
facing the wrong way
– towards what he was leaving –
dragged, against all the resistance
he could muster, a mess of entrails in his wake,
all torn and bleeding.

But over the last weeks he has lain
as if under a warm quilt,
and on that quilt a cat
treading continually,
each paw in turn sunk in
over and over, pressing and pushing,
making of him its own soft place,
a comfortable bed
on which to curl and sleep.

And in a pleasant confusion he wonders
whether that which he once called God
was the cat preparing to bed down
in the soft place of himself
or whether in fact *he* was the cat,
preparing to sink in
to the welcome of what he had once called God,
or heaven, or something.

Tent

Then he saw that in life
he had been a kind of tent,
stretched out, guy-ropes pegged taut
to the sides of a hill that caught the morning sun
and every kind of weather. Often
the wind and rain would buffet the canvas sides,
pushing and pummelling the tent like a lump of dough.
Soaking and distressing it.
The pegs were his loves, or sometimes
not quite loves but entanglements, driven
through roots
deep into the earth.
                    By erosion of the soil
that held the pegs, deformation of the pegs themselves
and the keen wind
that wore at the ropes, he arrived
at a state in which there was nothing
to hold him down.
Those who saw him rise
said it was as if
a giant jellyfish had floated up
and hung there:
such colours, such waving softnesses
combing and combed by the air.

Calf

On the far side of the hedge that bounds the churchyard
a cow lifts her throat to the sky and softly lows
– *Mugit* –
while, careful with straps, the men are easing the coffin
down into the pit they've dug deep against the difficulty
of driving rain. The sheerness of the pit's sides
is threatened by the water. Lumps
break off. Fall in. *Mugit.*
Mugivit. Mugiebat. She lowed.
She was lowing.

Beyond – can you hear it? – the white roar
as the great glacier is unplugged
from her calf. The grief-struck cow
is lowing. Her orphaned calf,
helplessly removed and drifting, calls out
as she floats off into the unnamed bay
leaving the raw cliff of her mother.
Mugiverunt – what Virgil's cattle did
when their quick calves were taken.
The cows and their calves bellowed.

Ancient words from a dead language,
spoken centuries before you and me
or lives like ours were dreamed of.
They understand by standing under
this severing present – their lament a *cantus firmus*,
to hold this shocked, irregular grief
in a compassion that's simply having known
a pain like this so long ago. If I scoop deep
enough I might touch it, this sustenance
in old ground.

at the churchyard

We pass one another at the entrance
with no nod. Her, the thin woman
with straggling fair hair and a cellophaned clutch
of tall flowers, I walk past
to my grave – yours – to bring you a posy
of hellebore, snowdrops and daffodils,
picked from the garden we made together
you and I. They're for you. For the place
where your body is actively ceasing
to be you. Becoming the place.

For at first what lay in the ground was you.
I'd call it you. I'd visit you there.
Then your body began
to be almost an 'it'
– the mortal remains – till
as the microbes and worms set to
their work of dismemberment
and digestion, that stuff becomes plural:
a teeming crowd, subject
to ever greater multiplication.

I go into the church to sit with you –
my thoughts of you – and soon I hear
someone else there. The thin woman.
This time, our flowers laid down, we can admit
the presence of the other. She's in tears –
her mother. Nearly a year now. I too, in tears.
We stand there, side by side and weeping,
still separate, differently mourning, though the composition
of our tears defies distinction as they stream, racing
into the common gutter.

Can you see?

Two brown hares,
belting – no, *haring*
across the claggy
ploughed field.
At the sight of me
they freeze
and disappear – brown
against the brown
peaked mud.

What else is there?
This wet, gleaming earth
like a picture
in a children's comic,
stuffed full of hidden objects
for a reader to make out:
a ball, a trumpet, a cricket bat
a Christmas tree,
a spinning top.

What else might be going on
in this monotonous, teeming ground?

The Sea of Tears

First she cried a basinfull
and remembered the puddings they'd made in it,
steamed for hours, to eat together.

Then she filled the mixing bowl
– the big one he used to knead dough
for their bread.

Next was the bath in which, at the beginning,
they'd washed and splashed
and examined one another with pleasure.

But the tears wouldn't stop. No man-made
container could hold them:
they streamed into the spring
that fed the lake
that fed the river
that poured into the sea
till the sea flooded and became
orginal Ocean.

Church bells
and the roar of commerce
can sometimes be heard
beneath these waters
on which she floats, mate-less,
within the Ark of Continuing Creatures.

Her companions include
a charred wallaby,
a pair of monitor lizards,
two porcupines
and a tethered
white parakeet.

It Takes so Little

The distance between us is so thin.
I can see your mouths pressing against the air,
opening and closing, like the hard,
handbag-clasp mouths of fishes
thrusting through the surface of the water to be fed.
'Keep back,' I want to say, 'Don't crowd me so.
All in good time. Don't worry,
I know you're there.' Oh I do.

It takes so little.
It used to be that in intercession
I'd lay your names out steadily,
like a person playing patience;
turn each card up to face the light,
and watch you – each one of you –
bloom and swell like a lantern flame
till you stood there,
clear as daylight.

But now I have only to think
your names and you're here,
plucking at me,
trying to show me something,
fussy and clamorous
in your eager dumbshows.

There should be a language
where naming is nothing
but blessing, and in no way
a summons: a mood where the living
and the also living are able to stay
in their places, and brim there
with strong satisfaction of being.

70

I don't want ever
to want not to think of you.
I don't ever want you
to go away.

He Rose Up

You know those dreams in which it is not
your childhood home. It shares no single
identifying feature with that home,
and yet is it. You know it, feel its welcome,
its complete familiarity; dreams in which
your mother, father, brother, dead friend
walk with you, and look nothing
like they looked before – but like a lion
or a tree or the woman from the bakery.
But you know what they are. They are they. Your heart
confirms it.

So it was with the Lord when he came to us
after the execution and burial. You could count those times
on one hand: they were ordinary –
walking and eating with us.
He did not look as he used to look
but he felt like him. Our hearts burned
when he spoke and broke our bread.
They burned as they only had
when he did those things. We knew him,
we handled him. He was real
as I am now.

The waters of Lake Tiberias were real too. They made
him wet as he waded there and handled the creel
of fish that – incredibly – we landed.
The weight of them! Thousands
of thrashing, whacking, silver and rainbow bodies,
the living meat that fed hungry us and all there. That weight
still present as he drew himself up into all
that lay over, pulling himself up into the lake
of the sky, puncturing heaven so that heaven poured down

and fell on us, gentle as a net that's flung loose and wide
to rest on the surface of the waters.

Pen

Her cob is dead
and cannot guard
the nest as he used to.

Her body a compact
white knot
against the cold

as she pushes her beak
deep into the pit
of a wing

and her down
underfeathers
keep warm

and in safety
the treasure
he fathered.

The New

Every one flips back the lid of a coffin
to climb out clean;
or they're like broad beans, fresh-thumbed
from silky, fur-lined pods:
these dear, blanched souls
with innocent rounded bellies,
naked and unashamed
as with beautiful washed feet they press
the unprintable turf of Paradise.

As a Vesture Shalt Thou Change Them
(Ps. 102:27)

Twenty two years, and he's back.
Entirely recognisable, but altered
from the state he was in when he left
when he was *Quite frankly*
said Clara, *a mess.*

Now, no mess, but sleek
and trim, freshly shaved, no stubble
but a soft cheek that smelled clean
so you'd want
to plant a kiss.

Clothes too, impeccable.
A jacket – dark blue. Cashmere
tailored to perfection.
She had to stroke it
and he allowed the caress.

On waking, it was the feel
of that wool that stayed with her,
as if a piece had got caught in the teeth
of Sheol's again-closing gates
leaving her this.

'the shag dips'

the shag dips
himself into absence
periscope withdrawn
leaving the water
poker-faced

it is impossible to guess
where along the wide
and flowing surface
of the water
he will surface

and I picture him
thickening that water
a darkness in the dark
through which the arrow
of him presses on

'At the School of the Tao they taught us'

At the School of the Tao they taught us
to use eyes differently and see
not the trunk or the boughs or the leaves of the tree
but the space in between: the sky
so fretted and framed.

Two identical dark profiles
press on a white candlestick.
The trick is to toggle the gaze between.
Since we must, let's make absence the thing:
that pillar of light.

Fusiform

Ubi

    Ubi

        Ubi

calls the owl
the question lies
on the air
and grows thin

you're not here
in bed to the left of me
or in your chair
at the kitchen table
you're not cycling or walking
soon to be home

                  you're not
even in the ground
where the dear
stuff that performed you
unravels and is
thoughtlessly being
unpicked and repurposed

only here
in a muscle
of mind
are you safe
and most portable
a spindle
that pulses and flares

Last Meal

They asked him to choose the food he liked best
for the eve of the execution.
They felt good about this, offering
a sop to take his mind off what was to come.

Sirloin and fries were usual,
then chocolate chip ice cream, with sprinkles.
But he did not want blood – or blubber – in his mouth.
There had already been too much killing.

Would the meal remain in his stomach
when he voided his bowels as they'd told him he might?
To be safe he chose words that would fill only his mouth –
words he could think and speak: cloud-berries,

picked from the Arctic tundra by his late mother;
samphire, pulled live from the peat at the edge of the salt marsh;
wild strawberries, their sweet white flesh, shy under leaves
at the edge of the forest; cheese from the milk

of cattle pastured on a mountain's green flank.
He wanted to hold it all in his mouth: the clouds, the snow,
the sea and its tributary rivers.
The mountains, the forests, the whole sky.

when the stars threw down their spears

fine needles
from sky
to earth
and back

or thick
as stair rods

hazel catkins
in perfect
pale verticals
and willow

weeps straight down
with no sorrow

as chimney sweepers come to dust

Not the soot-clad child
of William Blake
who cried *weep weep*
but a dandelion clock
each ensphered head
an airy globe
of fine umbrellaed
lances
        They shoot
and drift
        on breeze
and wind
        or ride
still air
        Their broadcast seed
grows everywhere

Notes for *When I Kiss the Sky*

Exemplum
Meister Eckhart (1260–c1327); German mystic and theologian

The Young Palaeontologist
Mary Anning (1799–1847) discovered the first ichthyosaurus fossil. She lived in Lyme Regis, as did I.

Edmund in Edmundsbury
This poem was written in 2015 at the end of a year as Writer in Residence at St Edmundsbury Cathedral. Its intention is to bind the story of Edmund King and Martyr (841–869) with the contemporary life of the cathedral dedicated to him. Some details are explained here that may be obscure to those unfamiliar with the town.

the sweet sugar-beet on its way to the factory: the British Sugar factory near the entrance to the town is a familiar landmark, puffing smoke when in action

From strength issued sweetness: see *Judges* 14, the riddle given to Samson and the motto on Tate and Lyle Golden Syrup tins

Samson: not the Scriptural Samson but Abbot Samson of Bury St Edmunds (1182–1211)

Greene King: the brewery is located in the town

Stephen Dykes Bower (1903–1994): architect responsible for extending the parish church of St James into St Edmundsbury cathedral

Shelley: the Suffolk parish (not the poet)

Goff: Leonard Goff, creator of two carved wooden statues in the cathedral; Elisabeth Frink's statue of a more warrior-like Edmund is outside, in the cathedral grounds

The Arc: a shopping centre in Bury St Edmunds

Cabinet cake: a speciality of the cathedral refectory in my day

Calf
the great glacier: Thwaites Glacier in West Antarctica is calving icebergs at an unprecedented rate, causing global sea levels to rise

Fusiform
Ubi the question asked by the owl in John Piper's Nativity window at the church of St Mary the Virgin, Iffley